TABLE OF CONTENTS

I0410819

ACRONYMS

CALL	Center for Army Lessons Learned
CJTF	Combined Joint Task Force
CPA	Coalition Provisional Authority
DHS	Department of Homeland Security
DoD	Department of Defense
DoS	Department of State
FBI	Federal Bureau of Investigation
GDP	Gross Domestic Product
HNPA	Host Nation Police Advising
ICITAP	International Criminal Investigative Training Assistance Program
IPTF	International Police Training Force
ITAM	Iraq Training and Advisory Mission
JCSFA	Joint Center for Security Force Assistance
MoI	Ministry of Interior
NATO	North Atlantic Treaty Organization
NSC	National Security Council
OPDAT	Office of Overseas Prosecutionary Development and Training
PKSOI	Peace Keeping and Stability Operations Institute
SFA	Security Force Assistance
SOFA	Status of Forces Agreement
USAID	United States Agency for International Development

TABLES

INTRODUCTION

Since America's first foreign war in Mexico in 1846, military leaders have faced the problem of deteriorating security and lawlessness that follow the battle.[1] Following the Mexican American War, the United States of America continued to enter numerous wars and conflicts. Yet the nation's military leaders still face the same unsolved issues of enforcing law and order during and especially after conflict ends. Although, there have been numerous solutions to enforcing law during and after war since the Mexican war, only some of them have proven enduring. This research examines two successful cases of rebuilding police forces in order to determine if the U.S. Military used the right formula in Iraq. This research is intended to assist in gleaning lessons should the United States commit to advising a police force in the future. Some of the questions this research seeks to answer are: What are the best means for the United States to rebuild a local, regional, or national police force for peacekeeping operations during or following a war? Does the police force determine the success of building rule of law? What role do police play in the building and maintaining of a successful nation?

The U.S. Army has focused a significant amount of effort in recent years toward forming the foundations of Security Force Assistance doctrine. Of all of the Joint Center for Security Force Assistance (JCSFA) and the Center for Army Lessons Learned (CALL) published handbooks, there is minimal U.S. Army doctrine written on this subject. Initial research into the roles of police assistance finds a significant discourse prescribing where and when the employment of the military in police building and security reform. For instance, the United States Agency for International Development (USAID) has the primary responsibility for mentoring and providing assistance to other national police forces as America's role of security force assistance.

---

[1]Timothy D. Johnson, *A Gallant Little Army: the Mexico City Campaign* (Lawrence : University Press of Kansas, 2007).

However, USAID and the State Department do not have the manning necessary to provide enough partnering capacity to meet the needs of police mentorship. As USAID does not have the manning necessary, the U.S. Army and the Military Police have fulfilled this role. This is not a new role, as the United States recently rebuilt many police forces in countries such as Germany, Japan, the Philippines, and Iraq.

This research assumes that a police force is the best security force as opposed to a military force for the success of a nation. This assumption was formed on a recent review of corruption within the country of Georgia. According to the *Geopolitical Monitor*, Georgia is an important example that has focused on police reforms and has subsequently grown their GDP since 2004.[2] As noted in this research, Georgia was successful because its leadership was able to limit the level of corruption in the public sector, particularly the police force.[3] Essentially, the president fired most of the police force then instituted harsh anti-corruption laws that jailed police officers who accepted bribes, while simultaneously reinvesting tax dollars into the police salary and infrastructure.[4] The correlating effect of these changes resulted in substantial decreases in corruption. In less than eight years, Georgia ranked 64th in the Corruption Index as opposed to their 2003 ranking of 124th.[5]

If the Georgian police can make a large impact in a short amount of time based on police professionalism and rule of law, then one can assume within transitory phases of operations that a

---

[2]Zachary Fillingham. "Nation Building & Police Reform: Lessons from Georgia."*Geopolitical Monitor*, July 2012, http://www.geopoliticalmonitor.com/nation-building-policereform-lessons-from-georgia-4696 (accessed 3 December 2012); Gapminder World. December 2,2012. http://www.gapminder.org/world/ (accessed 2 December 2012).

[3]Zachary Fillingham. "Nation Building & Police Reform: Lessons from Georgia."*Geopolitical Monitor*, July 2012, http://www.geopoliticalmonitor.com/nation-building-policereform-lessons-from-georgia-4696 (accessed 3 December 2012).

[4]Ibid.

[5]Ibid.

U.S. constabulary advising has a chance to advise a police force for the better. Therefore, the scope of this study will assess police involvement and constabulary advising functions gathered through various data and case study analysis that outline whether these actions have assisted other post-conflict nations in their development of effective police formations.

Additionally, the premise of the research recognizes that a nation can exist without a strong or community type police force. However, the analysis will seek to show that the success of a nation is dependent on the success of the police. Community policing values the level of involvement of the community and the proactive approach a police force takes to solve community problems.[6] A nation can still exist without a community police force, however what is required is that the nation must be able to police itself. In most cases, this is an unfeasible option.

LITERATURE REVIEW

In order to conduct an analysis on the U.S. capabilities for police force assistance, there must be a contextual framework of the history prior to the U.S. Army Security Force Assistance (SFA) missions in Iraq and Afghanistan. This contextual framework is not limited to history as it also reviews current U.S. policies regarding the SFA mission. In addition to this contextual framework, this foundation incorporates the review of common theoretical proposals for the actions of integrating and utilizing police forces during and after conflicts.

United States police advising and constabulary assistance has numerous examples, as well as a deep historical evolution; however, this study limits historical timeline from the latter half of the 20th Century to actions in 2012. This involves examining the evolution of history of

---

[6]Bureau of Justice Assistance, "Understanding Community Policing: A Framework for Action," *Community Policing Consortium* (Washington, D.C.: U.S. Department of Justice,1994),1-82; Robert R. Friedmann, William J. Cannon, "Homeland Security and Community Policing: Competing or Complementing Public Safety Policies,"*Journal of Homeland Security and Emergency Management* 4, no. 4, (2007), 1-23.

American police assistance and a review of the recommendations for American assistance in post-major conflict operations.

The United States developed numerous changes to their post-conflict approach throughout history, however, there are several themes that remain constant. A central theme is the requirement to transfer police functions to host nation forces as quickly as possible. For instance, various resources and theorists argue that a capable police force is necessary for the success of a nation.[7] Accordingly, much of the research will delve into the question surrounding the importance of developing an effective police force as a means to stabilize a nation and its institutions. This research will also examine how America can assist other national police forces in their endeavors without presenting solutions that are solely western focused.

Current publications commonly argue that the success of a nation is conditional upon the police. For example, David Galula advocates that a nation's police force is essential to the defense of a country during an insurgency.[8] He advocates the necessity of the police force in *Counter-Insurgency Warfare Theory and Practice* by formulating ideas that are based on the culmination of his involvement in several insurgencies in China, Greece, Vietnam, and Algiers while serving in the French Army.[9] Galula further elaborates the necessity to utilize the police, asserting there are three factors to police success: resources, police loyalty to the government, and the support of

---

[7]David Galula. *Counter-Insurgency Warfare: Theory and Practice* (New York: Frederick A. Praeger, Inc.,1964); James K. Wither, "Challenges of Developing Host Nation Police Capacity," *Prism* 3, no 4 (2012): 39-53; Casey, George W. *Strategic Reflections: Operation Iraqi Freedom* (Washington, D.C.:National Defense University Press, 2012); Zachary Fillingham, "Nation Building & Police Reform: Lessons from Georgia," *Geopolitical Monitor*, (July 2012), http://www.geopoliticalmonitor.com/nation-building-policereform-lessons-from-georgia-4696 (accessed 3 December 2012); Seth G. Jones, *Establishing Law and Order After Conflict* (Santa Monica, CA: Rand Publishing, 2005).

[8]David Galula, *Counter-Insurgency Warfare: Theory and Practice* (New York: Frederick A. Praeger Inc.,1964), 24.

[9]Ann Marlowe, "David Galula: His Life and Intellectual Context" (Monograph, U.S. War College, 2010).

a strong judicial system. Galula also advocates that the police are the "eye and arm of the government."[10] From this point of view, British counter-insurgency doctrine advocates police forces as an essential element to a nation, and they encourage the quick transition of military support to civilian authorities and their police.[11]

In addition to Galula's promotion of the police, former Multi-National Forces Iraq Commander, General George Casey, repeatedly advocated transitioning from external security forces to police forces.[12] In General Casey's *Strategic Reflection,* he discussed the growth and progression of shaping the Iraqi Police force into a community policing force.[13] He concretely advocates the successful counter-insurgency operations practice of placing the police in front of the military.[14] He formulated his ideas for advocating police assistance during his tenure in the Balkans.[15]

In another example, the United Nations involvement in the Balkans marked a transition in the Police Advising Roles of forces, particularly military. Prior to the Balkans intervention, most police advising and assistance was a reporting function. Nonetheless, recent peacekeeping roles have reshaped the views of police assistance.[16] For instance, Casy noted that, "in the last

---

[10]David Galula, *Counter-Insurgency Warfare: Theory and Practice* (New York: Frederick A. Praeger Inc.,1964), 24.

[11]James K. Wither, "Challenges of Developing Host Nation Police Capacity," *Prism* 3, no 4 (2012), 39.

[12]George W. Casey, *Strategic Reflections: Operation Iraqi Freedom* (Washington, D.C.: National Defense University Press, 2012), 51.

[13]Ibid., 38.

[14]Ibid., 45.

[15]Ibid., 58.

[16]James K. Wither, "Challenges of Developing Host Nation Police Capacity," *Prism* 3, no 4 (2012), 40.

fifteen years, policing operations have become increasingly complex with the requirement to undertake executive policing functions and often the major reform of the police."[17]As the UN represents the world in promoting police assistance, the roles and formulas for success continue to evolve. The UN has also promoted a policy of democratic policing.[18] Democratic policing ensures the force is responsible for protection of human rights.[19]

Democratic policing may be the policy the United Nations promotes, however, the United States is responsible for its own policies. The police force is the foundation to the society. Police represent the level of society which successfully inculcates rule of law. In 2004, USAID identified one of their five critical strategic goals for a fragile state as the establishment of rule of law that promotes human rights in concert with civilian police.[20] Accordingly, USAID's subsequent 2005 policy and guidance highlighted this requisite force in their democratic police force strategic goals. USAID's policy also highlighted that the goal for advising a democratic police force only applied to fragile states that were already a democracy.[21] Hence, we can infer that this goal does not apply to transitioning countries that are not under established democratic rule. The Peace Keeping and Stability Operations Institute (PKSOI) paper on *U.S. Military Forces and Police Assistance in Stability Operations*, discusses that police services are required

---

[17]James K. Wither, "Challenges of Developing Host Nation Police Capacity," *Prism* 3, no 4 (2012), 40.

[18]Ibid., 41.

[19]Ibid., 42.

[20]United States Agency for International Development, *Assistance for Civilian Policing.* USAID Policy Guidance, 2005,v.

[21]Ibid., vi.

for the success of a nation.[22] This paper also discussed the fact that the State Department is not manned nor are they willing to go into a country that is volatile or transitioning its government and rule of law.[23] Therefore, the author begrudgingly recognizes Military Police and Military Forces must fulfill the stability requirements post conflict. The author rationalizes the use of the military as the U.S. State Department can not provide extensive police advising programs in a non-permissive or transiting government.

The common trend post conflict is to promote a democratic or a community policing force and to transition security rapidly to these elements. Differences of opinion, however, revolve around the composition of the deployed force. Additionally, discourse has often prescribed the structure of the advisory forces as opposed to the descriptive nature this research wishes to achieve. The European Union (EU) did attempt to set the precedence in structuring a deployable advising force. According to the European Union (EU) in 2000, there was a goal to establish a rapid reaction force of police officers amongst the EU countries.[24] Although they promoted the idea, their deployment force fell 35% short of their manning goal.[25] This example demonstrates a prescriptive police advisory force will struggle when the deployment is secondary to completing their primary police obligations at home.

Promoting a prescriptive police advising force appears to be ideal; however the U.S. policy has directed multiple changes that have prevented a formation of this type of force. For instance, established in 1961, the International Cooperation Administration would eventually

---

[22]David E. Keller, *U.S. Military Forces and Police Assistance in Stability Operations: the least-Worst Option to fill the U.S. Capacity Gap* (Carlisle: Strategic Studies Institute, 2010), iii.

[23]Ibid., iii.

[24]James K. Wither, "Challenges of Developing Host Nation Police Capacity," *Prism 3,* no 4 (2012), 42.

[25]Ibid., 42.

evolve into the U.S. Agency for International Development (USAID).[26] "In 1963, USAID would establish the International Police Academy in Washington, DC, to train," advise, and equip foreign police officers.[27] In essence, if American leadership had followed this unfolding organizational path and subsequently laid the proper institutional framework in the 1960s, there would not be a need for this research. The Senate committee on Foreign Relations Report, published in August of 1973 preceded the Foreign Assistance Act of 1974 and would forever change USAID's involvement in training other national police. In essence, this report outlined a proposal for closing the USAID training program because of a stigma attached by accusations of that their agency trained police that were associated with allegations of brutality.[28] The context shaping the congressional report depended upon the drawdown of the U.S. Army in that era and political pressures following the Vietnam War. One can infer that this led to a backlash against federalized or mandated police advising. The USAID decentralization of police force assistance in the 1970s following Section 660 of the Foreign Assistance Act of 1974 by the U.S. Congress, led to a disjointed strategy for U.S. national host nation police advising post-conflict.[29]

Since the dismantling of the USAID centralized training program in 1974, there have been a number training programs established throughout the federal government but funded primarily through USAID. The PKSOI paper notes that there is a small Department of State, International Narcotics and Law Enforcement Bureau, that provides a minor role in training other

[26]David E. Keller, *U.S. Military Forces and Police Assistance in Stability Operations: the least-Worst Option to fill the U.S. Capacity Gap* (Carlisle: Strategic Studies Institute, 2010), 3; Melissa M. Cantwell, "Evolution of Both Host Nation Police Advisory and the Support Provided by the Department of Defense" (Master's thesis, School of Advanced Military Studies, 2012), 4.

[27]David E. Keller, *U.S. Military Forces and Police Assistance in Stability Operations: the least-Worst Option to fill the U.S. Capacity Gap* (Carlisle: Strategic Studies Institute, 2010), 5.

[28]Ibid.,7.

[29]Ibid., 6.

national police.[30] Most of the other programs are in the Department of Justice, which established

minimal international training programs funded by the State Department such as the International

Criminal Investigative Training Assistance Program (ICITAP).[31] Military operations in Panama

expanded the ICITAP in 1989.[32] As these programs grew, they expanded to meet the growing

needs and changes in U.S. Strategy. In order to accomplish this the Office of Overseas

Prosecutionary Development and Training (OPDAT) and the Offices of Civilian Police and Rule

of Law Programs were established.[33] Even with this growing enterprise, USAID remained limited

to funding small programs. In fact, the 2005 Foreign Operations, Export Financing and Related

Programs Appropriations Act was the United States Congress's first attempt to grant USAID

authority "to conduct police training on a worldwide basis."[34]

Although the State Department closed their International Police Academy in 1974,

USAID still issues policy guidance as it pertains to working with civilian police authorities.[35]

The USAID policy cites program goals for a "civilian police authority which means a public

safety or constabulary force" and community-based policing that is "a partnership between the

police and the community they serve."[36] This guidance issued after Congress passed section

564(a) of the Foreign Operations, Export Financing, and Related Programs Appropriations Act in

---

[30]David E. Keller, *U.S. Military Forces and Police Assistance in Stability Operations: the least-Worst Option to fill the U.S. Capacity Gap* (Carlisle: Strategic Studies Institute, 2010), 7.

[31]Ibid., 8.

[32]Ibid., 10.

[33]Ibid., 12.

[34]Ibid., 11.

[35]United States Agency for International Development, *Assistance for Civilian Policing,* USAID Policy Guidance, 2005, v.

[36]Ibid.

2005. The PKSOI paper illustrated that although there is not a sole institution that trains and conducts HNPA; USAID still issues the guidance, as well as funds multiple programs in order to facilitate U.S. police advisory. This 2005 act followed changes in Iraq's Coalition Provisional Authority to transfer responsibilities of organizing, training, and equipping the Iraqi Police to Iraq's Ministry of Interior.[37] Unfortunately, the hierarchal transfer of responsibility did not alleviate the Department of Defenses advisory program despite intentions to use the program to transform the Iraqi police into a community police force.[38] USAID further elaborated this community-based policing in goals to "establish the rule of law, with security and human rights protections as an inherent component of a democratic political order" in order to enable free trade and commerce.[39] The essence of the policy is USAID will only fund and promote assistance for countries that are working toward democracy.

As USAID expands, it still relies on funding through the federal government. For example, the Department of Homeland Security now has an International Law Enforcement Academy and organized Customs and Border Patrol advisory missions in Central America and Iraq.[40] The PKSOI paper elaborates that the reason USAID must fund these various noncontiguous programs resides in the fact that the "United States lacks the institutional capacity to provide an immediate and coordinated civilian police training and advisory effort, particularly

---

[37]Office of the Special Inspector General for Iraq Reconstruction United States Government, *Iraqi Police Development Program: Opportunities for Improved Program Accountability and Budget Transparency* (Arlington: State Department, 2011), 1.

[38]Casey, George W. *Strategic Reflections: Operation Iraqi Freedom* (Washington, D.C.: National Defense University Press, 2012), 39-51.

[39]United States Agency for International Development, *Assistance for Civilian Policing,* USAID Policy Guidance, 2005, v.

[40]David E Keller, *U.S. Military Forces and Police Assistance in Stability Operations: the least-Worst Option to fill the U.S. Capacity Gap* (Carlisle: Strategic Studies Institute, 2010).

in a failed or fragile state."[41] Although the United States and USAID lack the institutional capacity, the PKSOI paper proclaims that the Military must be prepared to train.[42] This research further outlines that the U.S. Military and Military Police are not trained in community policing methods, making the U.S. Military and Military Police are the "*least worst option*" for America to employ in time of war.[43]

Another Department of Defense (DoD) evaluation following the conflicts in Kosovo, Haiti, and Panama determined successes and failures in host nation police assistance.[44] For instance, as outlined in her 2012 study, Melissa Cantrell determined that although there were successes in Kosovo and Panama, the DoD did not plan for the process of police advising.[45] She further indicates that there is not an overarching strategy for these deployments, nor is there an established structure to conduct these missions in the future.[46] Cantrell does propose, however, that the United States Military Police Corps continuess executing these types missions as there are proposals to adjust the structure of the deploying force in order to provide additional skill sets, like more investigators.[47]

From these arguments, two common themes arise. First, there is still a requirement to provide police force assistance and secondly this force should provide assistance to build a

---

[41]David E Keller, *U.S. Military Forces and Police Assistance in Stability Operations: the least-Worst Option to fill the U.S. Capacity Gap* (Carlisle: Strategic Studies Institute, 2010), viii.

[42]Ibid., viii.

[43]Ibid.

[44]Melissa M. Cantwell, "*Evolution of Both Host Nation Police Advisory and the Support Provided by the Department of Defense*" (Master's Thesis, School of Advanced Military Studies, 2012).

[45]Ibid., 54.

[46]Ibid., 63.

[47]Ibid., 61-62.

democratic or community police as a part of building a democratic society. What is still not clear is what type of force is necessary to conduct these nation-building efforts. Although the composition is not conclusive, it appears most authors agree that the military or a military like-force is going to be the first deployed to a region to set up a police force even if it is not the ideal option.

The military is likely to be the first force sent into a theater of operations following a major armed conflict. This military presence, in turn, is derived from the assumption that the U.S. Military Police Corps would be the first to provide assistance to a nation's police force. To assess this assumption, a historical look at the U.S. Military Police Corps is necessary.

The lineage of the modern U.S. Military Police Corps dates back to the Revolutionary War, however it is during WWII that the U.S. Army received its first Provost Marshal and established the Military Police Corps as a branch.[48] Although the establishment correlated to the onset of WWII and the United States fears of espionage, the corps received more than subversive acts to investigate. The U.S. Military Police assumed duties to investigate and report the crimes under the uniform code of military justice.[49] Of particular note is the fact that initial duties did not include constabulary advisement of a foreign police force.

As the United States entered the war in WWII, the Military Police Branch was tasked with traffic control on the battlefield.[50] Although the core duties of the military police officer had not officially changed, they were quickly expanding into guarding prisoners of war and eventually guarding rear areas.[51] As the U.S. invasion forces moved across Europe these roles

---

[48]Robert K. Wright, *Military Police* (Washington, D.C.: Center of Military History, 1992), 10.

[49]Ibid., 10.

[50]Ibid., 11.

[51]Ibid., 11.

transitioned quickly to policing towns in order to maintain a level of order by preventing looting

and other crimes. After the war, the U.S. Military Police Corps fulfilled its duties of guarding

prisoners of war awaiting trial. Eventually the military police provided assistance in the form of

provost marshal sections to U.S. Calvary brigades and battalions as these units conducted police

advising. Throughout the Vietnam War, Military Police gained larger combat roles. One Military

Police unit even served as a landowner, which was a job predominantly held by combat troops

like Infantry and Armor.[52] These tasks were in addition to their traditional responsibilities of law

enforcement and prisoner guarding functions. The post- Iraq Invasion adapted these Military

Police roles again as they assumed host nation police advising missions. As host nation police

advising missions were not primary responsibilities of the Military Police, the case studies put

forth will investigate the development of this role through the Department of Defense's post-

conflict involvement.

RESEARCH METHODOLOGY

The intent of this research is to look at correlating lessons from selected case studies to

determine if the United States constabulary advising has changed the nation's post-conflict

situation. More importantly, this insight is necessary in order to define whether Military Police

Corps advising has been more effective than that of historical constabulary advising or State

Department sponsored policing missions. Firstly police advising often illustrates a prescriptive

nature for employing advisory forces. Several of the literature review sources advocated the

military and military police should be used as this requisite force as there isn't an USAID force to

deploy in the times of need following a conflict. [53] These sources are great if needed, but is there

---

[52]Robert K. Wright, *Military Police* (Washington, D.C.: Center of Military History, 1992), 12.

[53] David E. Keller, *U.S. Military Forces and Police Assistance in Stability Operations: the least-Worst Option to fill the U.S. Capacity Gap* (Carlisle: Strategic Studies Institute, 2010);

a question missing? When should a military be employed as a host nation advisory force, and is there circumstances that could lead decision makers to understand when the United States should and should not use the military versus a USAID advisory element? There have been instances where the military have not been the primary advisory force. The literature review left the author without a descriptive understanding for when it is necessary to employ these types of forces. This study will define military police involvement and constabulary advising functions and determine through a review and case study analysis whether these actions have assisted the other nations post-conflict. Regardless if the constabulary force is primarily democratic, human rights protective, or geared toward a proactive community policing, this research focuses on determining the implementation of a military vice civilian force for the success of stability in nation-building operations.

The hypothesis for this research is that a police force is necessary for the success of the nation and Military Police are a more effective force for the initial stages of nation building. In order to provide evidence for this argument, this research will compare three nations that the United States has assisted in securing and rebuilding. These three nations are Germany, Bosnia, and Iraq. These countries have had varying degrees of United States economic and police involvement in their nations following periods of conflicts. Critical analysis will be conducted on the roles that either the DoS or the DoD played in the reconstruction periods against the study's defined level of success.

To examine the three nations, this research assesses the nation's pre-war and post-war policing structure. There is not a specific benchmark that each nation is evaluated against, rather

---

United States Agency for International Development, *Assistance for Civilian Policing,* USAID Policy Guidance, 2005; James K. Wither, "Challenges of Developing Host Nation Police Capacity" *Prism* 3, no 4 (2012), 39-53; George W. Casey, *Strategic Reflections: Operation Iraqi Freedom* (Washington, D.C.: National Defense University Press, 2012); Melissa M. Cantwell, *"Evolution of Both Host Nation Police Advisory and the Support Provided by the Department of Defense"* (Master's Thesis, School of Advanced Military Studies, 2012), 11.

the analysis weighs the improvement that the host nation advising police force made in each of the countries. This evaluation is necessary to determine if the nation improved after U.S. police or constabulary involvement. This review does not preclude the need for further improvement, nor is the research going to conduct a measurement against the United Nation's benchmark of the Human Development Index for each country. Rather the assessment measures the length of time, government structure, and police structure improvement. These evaluations will be used to find correlations to U.S. host nation advising operations. Each nation entered into conflict with varying levels of democracy, therefore there is the possibility of correlating democracy to the U.S. operations, length of stay, and the success of the advising force.

In addition to varying country characteristics, the literature review derived the differences in the main article of evaluation host nation police advisory operations. The advisory force for each of the studies looks at the three types of compositions: constabulary (military), United Nations Civilian expertise, and Military Police with Civilian expertise. The case studies selected will also evaluate three different snapshots of the host nation police advising in order to link best practices. For instance, the first nation followed a multinational war, the second nation followed a civil war, and the third follows a Coalition invasion. All three of the police forces, however were different in both their composition and mission, and therefore, the contextual aspects of each solution that was put forth illustrates varying degrees of successful outcomes.

CASE STUDIES

All three case studies follow the following format: a description of the nation before and after the conflict, a depiction of the type of conflict that occurred, and the status of the nation at the transition into the stability phase. Further, the author seeks to understand the type of deployed police advisory force that was used during the mission (i.e. constabulary vice a community police advisory force), specialties in that force, the type of German police forces that existed before the conflict, and the type of German police force after the conflict.

15

Germany

Historically, Germany represents one of the best examples of the evolution of a police force during the development of a Police State. Although Germany was a democracy following WWI, the country slowly transitioned into a Police State as Adolf Hitler consolidated his power.[54] As an example of this transition, the Gestapo began using their new found powers by arresting various individuals to include Jews and other minorities as a means to segregate them from the "pure Aryan" population. Unfortunately, many of these people would disappear, never to be seen again. In essence, the police and criminal system evolved to reflect and support the many changes seen in Nazi Germany.[55] For instance, there was a rapid expansion of capital punishment that by 1936 included some 90 per cent of death sentences being passed by the courts. Prosecutors and courts were further encouraged to charge all homicides with murder rather than the non-capital offense of manslaughter required to reach a guilty verdict.[56] As harsher sentences for criminals increased, the system adapted. For example, criminals convicted of at least three lesser crimes were often subjected to retroactive sentencing and would likely die in prison.[57] This Police State enforcement ruled Germany with an unsympathetic sentiment of enforcement fueled by the Nazi regime. Not all embraced the new rules, however, as local political leaders that objected were fired and were replaced with politicians that would commiserate with the Nazi mentality.[58]

---

[54]Richard J. Evans, *The Third Reich in Power*, (New York, NY: Penguin Books, 2005), 75.

[55]Ibid.

[56]Ibid.

[57]Ibid., 76.

[58]Ibid., 77.

It would take several years for Allied forces to defeat the Nazis. In fact, the United States would resort to actions that have been characterized as "carpet bombing" in order to destroy city infrastructure, costing thousands of non-combatants lives.[59] United States Army planners developed the transition from Operation OVERLORD to Operation ECLIPSE pending the defeat of the Germans during the early 1940s. Throughout planning, American forces anticipated demobilization of the German military forces along with assuming government responsibilities and law enforcement.[60] However, in 1945 when Germany unconditionally surrendered the U.S. Military was faced with a total breakdown of the society.[61] Widespread crime and a desperate need for humanitarian assistance complicated the issues and implementation of the plans post World War II.[62]

Following WWII, on 8 May 1945, Germany's government was almost non-existent and the nation was filled with displaced civilians, which posed a significant disruption to social order.[63] The United States continued to conduct its sector occupation plan with the carrying out of martial law.[64] The U.S. Military implemented Operation ECLIPSE, which instituted a

---

[59] A.C. Grayling, *Among the Dead Cities: The History and Moral Legacy of the WWII Bombing Campaign of Civilians in Germany and Japan* (New York: Walker & Company, 2006).

[60]Kendall D. Gott and Combat Studies Institute, *Mobility, Vigilance, and Justice: the Us Army Constabulary in Germany 1946-1953* (Ft Leavenworth: Combat Studies Institute Press, 2005), 3; Oliver F. Frederiksen, *The American Military Occupation of Germany 1945-1953* (Heidelberg: US Army Europe Headquarters,1984), 1-2.

[61]*Mobility, Vigilance, and Justice: the Us Army Constabulary in Germany 1946-1953*, 2005, 6; *The American Military Occupation of Germany 1945-1953*, 1984, 65-66.

[62]Ibid.

[63]James M. Snyder, *Establishment operations of the U.S. Constabulary 3 October 1945 to 30 June 1947* (APO, Germany: U.S. Army, 1947),1; Kendall D. Gott and Combat Studies Institute, *Mobility, Vigilance, and Justice: the Us Army Constabulary in Germany 1946-1953* (Ft Leavenworth: Combat Studies Institute Press, 2005), 5.

[64]Historical Division European Command, *Reorganization of Tactical Forces VE-Day to 1 January 1949* (Karlsruhe, Germany:European Command, 1950),14.

Constabulary force to maintain law and order and quell any uprisings.[65] "It was expected that a

gradual reduction in the police-type duties of the constabulary would take place as the German

police force, customs service, railroad police, and other services became operational."[66]

The constabulary forces were more a stopgap measure until the national police could

begin full operations.[67] The advisory capacity was limited; however, the intent was to conduct the

initial vetting of the German Police, which met the standards for denazification while training

basic police duties.[68] The occupation of Germany resulted in the Military Police maintaining

order amongst the soldiers and an establishment of a separate constabulary force that secured the

population.[69] This force would ultimately be responsible for working with the constabulary to

conduct simultaneous law enforcement operations and border security for enforcing the U.S.

Zone.[70] The constabulary force structure mimicked that of the various U.S. state police forces.

Their primary mission began with law and order operations of German citizens in the absence of

rule of law.[71] The constabulary force conducted enforcement to prohibit the growing black

---

[65]Historical Division European Command, *Reorganization of Tactical Forces VE-Day to 1 January 1949* (Karlsruhe, Germany:European Command, 1950),14.

[66]Ibid., 21.

[67]James, Dobbins, John G. McGinn, Keith Crane, Seth G. Jones, Rollie Lal, Andrew Rathmell, Rachel Swanger, and Anga Timilsina, *America's Role in Nation-Building: From Germany to Iraq* (Santa Monica: RAND Corporation, 2003), 10.

[68]Ibid., 11.

[69]James M. Snyder, *Establishment operations of the U.S. Constabulary 3 October 1945 to 30 June 1947* (APO, Germany: U.S. Army, 1947), 8-9; Kendall D. Gott and Combat Studies Institute, *Mobility, Vigilance, and Justice: the Us Army Constabulary in Germany 1946-1953* (Ft Leavenworth: Combat Studies Institute Press, 2005), 10.

[70]Kendall D. Gott and Combat Studies Institute, *Mobility, Vigilance, and Justice: the Us Army Constabulary in Germany 1946-1953* (Ft. Leavenworth: Combat Studies Institute Press, 2005), 10.

[71]Ibid.

market and border issues that were arising with the establishment of the U.S. Zone of Germany.[72]

Each of these actions was to be synchronized with the growing and grooming of their German

counterparts.

Although the Americans had German counterparts, this was the first time in U.S. history

that the U.S. Army had instituted a force that was clearly delineated from its primary tactical

mission.[73] This force was an occupation force intended to maintain law and order.[74] This force

was also intended to restore Germany to the pre-Nazi government or democratic government

where they would remove weapons and make an effort to deactivate the Nazi military.[75]

The Constabulary force was primarily comprised of U.S. Calvary troops, with only an

addition of provost marshals later in the occupation.[76] There was contemplation and requests,

however, for the augmentation of additional troops from Denmark, Norway, Switzerland, France

and others.[77] Unfortunately, all plans were disbanded based on a lack of commitment from these

other nations leaving a primary American Constabulary force.[78] High turnover in forces, morale

issues, and a total troop ceiling of 300,000 instead of a planned 404,000 would mean the

---

[72]Kendall D. Gott and Combat Studies Institute, *Mobility, Vigilance, and Justice: the Us Army Constabulary in Germany 1946-1953* (Ft. Leavenworth: Combat Studies Institute Press, 2005),10.

[73]Historical Division European Command, *Reorganization of Tactical Forces VE-Day to 1 January 1949* (Karlsruhe, Germany: European Command, 1950), 1.

[74]James M. Snyder, *Establishment Operations of the U.S. Constabulary 3 October 1945 to 30 June 1947* (APO, Germany: U.S. Army, 1947), 4.

[75]Ibid.

[76]Ibid., 5.

[77]Historical Division European Command, *Reorganization of Tactical Forces VE-Day to 1 January 1949* (Karlsruhe, Germany: European Command, 1950), 10.

[78]Ibid.

constabulary force would never obtain their full goal of 39,000. [79] These figures were based on agreements found in the memos between General Eisenhower and General McNarney. [80]

There was an occupational struggle for balance in planning the missions of this constabulary force. The protection of Germany from the Communists had to balance with the policing functions necessary to maintain law and order. This would prove to be a persistent point of contention as units drew down after 1945. [81] The constabulary was "intended as a mobile reserve of tactical troops which would be capable of quick action; provide security coverage by patrolling; make searches for the apprehension of wanted persons and the recovery of contraband goods" as they were the enforcement and arrest authority link for the Counter-intelligence Corps. [82] Although some of these aspects appear to be police functions, the constabulary was not an extension of the German Rule of Law. Rather, the constabulary was the intermediary function for the host nation until the German force could be appropriately reequipped to enforce a democratic German Rule of Law.

Prior to World War II, Germany moved from a fragile democracy into a state that produced stringent law and order practices. The stringent practices and lack of transparency were apparent in the discourse between the public and police prior to 1945. [83] For example, prisoners

---

[79]Historical Division European Command, *Reorganization of Tactical Forces VE-Day to 1 January 1949* (Karlsruhe, Germany: European Command, 1950), 8, 28.

[80]Ibid., 4-9.

[81]Ibid., 4-13; Polish Displaced Civilians were used to augment US Military guards and assist in guarding important industry until 1947 when US decided to reduce this force. By 1948 mostly Germans served as industry police and worked under the U.S. Army.

[82]James M. Snyder, *Establishment Operations of the U.S. Constabulary 3 October 1945 to 30 June 1947*, (APO, Germany: U.S. Army, 1947), 6.

[83]Richard J. Evans, *The Third Reich in Power*, (New York, NY: Penguin Books, 2005) 75.

were often beaten and these actions were noticed.[84] In fact, the Justice Ministry found these

practices objectionable. They did not reflect well on the reputation of the law enforcement

apparatus in Germany. After a good deal of negotiation, a compromise was found at a meeting

held on 4 June 1937, when police and Justice Ministry officials agreed that such arbitrary

beatings should cease. Henceforth, the meeting ruled that police interrogators were to be limited

to administering twenty-five lashes to interviewees in the presence of a doctor, and they had to

use a 'standard cane' to do so.[85] These beatings were not a product of the society but rather the

indoctrination of the Nazi ruling party onto the society. Therefore, the onslaught of the war torn

nation destroyed the semblance of the rule of law and likely made the constabulary job easier to

return to a pre-Nazi status.

In order to return to a democratic society, the German police force would mimic the U.S.

state or county police structures and subsequently divide their forces among their cities and

communities.[86] The constabulary operations would begin gradually with the intention to be

operational in 1946.[87] It was also not until 1946, that the United States would allow the German

Police to go back into their jobs, and only after they understood they worked for the constabulary

which would have the broad mission of protecting American interests and personnel."[88] One year

later in 1947, the German Police were operating as a capable police force.[89]

---

[84]Richard J. Evans, *The Third Reich in Power* (New York: Penguin Books, 2005), 75.

[85]Ibid.

[86]Historical Division European Command, *Reorganization of Tactical Forces VE-Day to 1 January 1949* (Karlsruhe, Germany: European Command, 1950), 5-6; James M. Snyder, *Establishment operations of the U.S. Constabulary 3 October 1945 to 30 June 1947* (APO, Germany: U.S. Army, 1947), 3.

[87]James M. Snyder, *Establishment Operations of the U.S. Constabulary 3 October 1945 to 30 June 1947* (APO, Germany: U.S. Army, 1947), 12.

[88]Historical Division European Command, *Reorganization of Tactical Forces VE-Day to 1 January 1949,*(Karlsruhe, Germany: European Command, 1950), 5-6.

Understandably, the German Police were operating as a capable police force quickly, but the U.S. Military continued to have a presence. Therefore the evaluation of the U.S. Military stay in Germany varies by how one defines the length of the U.S. Military stay. The described occupation of the United States in Germany occurred from 1945 to 1952.[90] Although the occupation ended in 1952, there has been a presence of U.S. Soldiers there since WWII. Germany and the United States entered into their earliest Status of Forces agreement (SOFA) dated in 1951.[91] Therefore, evaluating the affect of the constabulary and military forces on Germany for this research requires a snapshot in time. The implementation of the SOFA is a safe measurement of effectiveness as the presumption is a nation that enforces a SOFA is a nation that is ready to assume the roles and responsibilities for securing their own society. Although there is still a presence of U.S. Military in the country of Germany, the length of evaluation only applies to the Military and constabulary forces from 1945 to 1952.

Bosnia

Prior to the Bosnia Herzegovina conflict in 1992, this communist nation which was approximately the size of Louisiana, had much of the modern infrastructure that many modern industrialized countries possess.[92] For instance, power, water, and sewage all were in good working order until the Bosnian Conflict began. The nation was also demographically dispersed

---

[89]Historical Division European Command, *Reorganization of Tactical Forces VE-Day to 1 January 1949,*(Karlsruhe, Germany: European Command, 1950), 29.

[90]Kendall D. Gott and Combat Studies Institute, *Mobility, Vigilance, and Justice: the Us Army Constabulary in Germany 1946-1953* (Ft. Leavenworth: Combat Studies Institute Press, 2005),1.

[91]R.Chuck Mason, *Status of Forces Agreement (SOFA), What Is It, and How Has it Been Utilized?* (Washington, D.C.: Congressional Research Service, 2009), 10.

[92]Larry K. Wentz, *Lessons from Bosnia* (Washington, D.C.: National Defense University Press, 1997), 10.

with large segments of Muslim, Croatian and Serbian Ethnicities cohabitating peacefully.[93] It was

not until Slovenia and Croatia declared independence from Yugoslavia in 1991 that this nation of

majority Muslims saw an internal and external ethnic struggle for their country.[94] This ethnic

struggle would change the cultural face of Bosnia as the Serbian Christian-based population

surpassed the Muslim population also resulting in massive destruction to infrastructure, cities, and

towns.[95]

This conflict ultimately resulted in the Dayton Peace Agreement, which required the

deployment of a North Atlantic Treaty Organization (NATO) command including a peacekeeper

force from throughout the United Nations.[96] The ethnic cleansing that was a part of this war

created "the largest number of refugees and displace people in Europe since World War II."[97] The

destruction was massive and extended beyond the government and the city of Sarajevo

encompassing all of Bosnia.[98] As the Dayton Accords went into effect, the NATO command

forces had to establish security for the humanitarian effort to succeed.

Establishing security was not an easy endeavor as enormous debate centered on the best

methods for standing up the police forces. The police force and accompanying rule of law under

the previous Yugoslavian controlled-government collapsed as a result of the existing police using

---

[93]Larry K. Wentz, *Lessons from Bosnia* (Washington, D.C.: National Defense University Press, 1997), 10.

[94]Ibid., 23.

[95]Ibid., 10-23.

[96]Ibid., 1.

[97]Kristen Young, "UNHRC and ICRC in the Former Yugoslavia, Bosnia-Herzegovina," RICR Septembre IRRC Vol. 83 No 843 (September 2001), 781.

[98]Larry K. Wentz, *Lessons from Bosnia* (Washington, D.C.: National Defense University Press, 1997), xxii.

their positions of authority to incite ethnic violence.[99] Therefore, any apparatus that became a part of the Bosnian rule of law had to consider the ethnic tensions when building a balanced representation of the country.

In accordance with the Dayton Accords, the peacekeeping forces began oversight of the Bosnian Military demobilization. After the peacekeeping forces began to realize the demobilization process was swelling the police force beyond the European standards, the process stopped.[100] The demobilization or the Armed Forces directly affected the Bosnian police forces. Their newly acquired military counter parts saturated the police culture by creating a shortage of law enforcement expertise amongst the ranks.[101]

The intended structure was a National Police force similar to the organization in place prior to the escalation of conflict. For instance, Bosnia and Herzegovina both had forces under the control of the Minister of Interior prior to the conflict.[102] The configuration divided into a common county-type where each of the ten Cantons had a smaller Ministry of Interior.[103] Not until 2002 would the Federal level receive an enforcement agency of their own, called the State information and Protection Agency.[104] This agency, that was intended for the enforcement of federal crimes and international terrorism, highlighted the disparate criminal differences and

---

[99]Larry K. Wentz, *Lessons from Bosnia* (Washington, D.C.: National Defense University Press, 1997), 13.

[100]Ibid., 14; The European Standard for police force ratio was one police officer per 330 persons, however the military that joined the Police resulted in exceeding that ratio.

[101]Ibid.

[102]ICMPD, *Financial, Organisational And Administrative Assessment Of The Bih Police Forces And The State Border Service*, (Sarajevo: European Union, 2004), 14.

[103]Ibid.

[104]Ibid.

added to a bureaucratic and uneven structure.[105] Although the original Ministry of Interior

administered over the internal Canton law enforcement, the added Bosnian State Information and

Protection Agency created an added ministry of security.[106] This additional ministry inhibited

coordination between the new agency and the Cantons.[107] These actions represent the possible

stove-piped information flow and actions of their current system.

The Dayton Accords mandated a democratic police structure in Bosnia following

hostilities. For example, the IPTF had to enforce "in accordance with internationally recognized

standards and with respect for internationally recognized human rights and fundamental

freedoms."[108] The International Police Task Force (IPTF) was responsible for ensuring the

Bosnian forces met this standard.[109] The IPTF was to advise and assist the Bosnian police forces

through a mentoring relationship in compliance with the Dayton Accords.[110] This mentoring

relationship met with resistance in some parts of Bosnia, as the republic of Serbia was not a part

in the Dayton Accords, and Serbians remained the largest ethnicity after the war.[111] The role of

the IPTF is distinctly different from that of the German post-conflict Constabulary of the 1940s,

---

[105]ICMPD, *Financial, Organisational And Administrative Assessment Of The Bih Police Forces And The State Border Service*, (Sarajevo: European Union, 2004), 14.

[106]Ibid.

[107]Ibid.

[108]IFOR, The General Framework Agreement: Dayton Accords Annex 4, Article III, 2 (c), http://www.nato.int/ifor/gfa/gfa-an1a.htm (accessed March 1, 2013).

[109]ICMPD, *Financial, Organisational And Administrative Assessment Of The Bih Police Forces And The State Border Service* (Sarajevo: European Union, 2004), 15.

[110]Ibid.

[111]Larry K. Wentz, *Lessons from Bosnia* (Washington D.C.: National Defense University Press, 1997), 152.

as they were not fulfilling a void. The task force, however, filled a direct training and advising mission from the beginning.

This task force ultimately answered to the United Nations and filled the IPTF through their UN volunteer program.[112] The International Police Task Force was part of the larger peacekeeping force that worked for NATO.[113] This force also included non-NATO members; however, it was primarily comprised of French, British, and United States Military members.[114] The force intended to provide one monitor for every 30 police officers, and they required prerequisites for these monitors.[115] The parameters prescribed for the mentors, were the requirement to speak English, drive and have eight years of law enforcement experience.[116] It took almost eight months to fulfill these requirements to advise the 44,750 police officers.[117] Due to the parameters and time constraints many argued that, "often the most neglected portion was the law enforcement experience."[118] Therefore, the monitors could advise the 44,750 police officers, many of whom had more law enforcement experience then their own. In 1996, to avoid further discrepancies of police force mentoring competencies, the UN began checking and testing

---

[112]Edward J Horgan, Assisting *or Hindering Democracy? International Intervention and The Democratization of Bosnia and Herzegovina* (Dissertation, Master of Philosophy in Peace Studies Irish School of Ecumenics), 21.

[113]Larry K. Wentz, *Lessons from Bosnia* (Washington D.C.: National Defense University Press, 1997), xix.

[114]Ibid., 2.

[115]Ibid., 142.

[116]Ibid., 143.

[117]Larry K. Wentz, *Lessons from Bosnia* (Washington D.C.: National Defense University Press, 1997), 142, 144-147. The IPTF was allotted 1700 police monitors. Logistics and recruiting issues led to delays in establishing the force. Of note, the author pointed out the United States also hesitated in fulfilling their requirements for the IPTF.

[118]Ibid., 143.

the IPTF monitors before they came to Bosnia.[119] Additional training and orientation classes implemented subsequently monitors could become familiar with some of the issues found in Bosnia, such as mines.[120]

Although the IPTF had humble beginnings, the recent descriptions of Bosnia Herznogovia illustrate a police force that is quite different from the recent past. IPTF provided mentorship until the end of the United Nations mission in December 2002.[121] Although the IPTF ended its official capacity in December of 2002, Bosnia entered into a SOFA agreement in 2005, making the length of stay ten years from the entrance of peacekeeping forces in 1995. Prior to the SOFA, Bosnia was reported as having public security services that were on par with European standards.[122] For example, response times for emergency calls rated as "5-10 minutes within urban areas and 15-50 minutes in rural areas."[123] Additionally, the victimization surveys conducted in 2001 stated "75% of the population felt secure" which was just slightly below Belgium or Switzerland rating.[124]

---

[119]Larry K. Wentz, *Lessons from Bosnia* (Washington D.C.: National Defense University Press, 1997),143.

[120]Ibid.,144.

[121]International Crisis Group, "Policing the Police in Bosnia: A Further Reform Agenda" (Balkans Report N°130, Sarajevo/Brussels, 10 May 2002), http://www.crisisgroup.org/en/regions/europe/balkans/bosnia-herzegovina/130-policing-the-police-in-bosnia-a-further-reform-agenda.aspx (accessed 3 March 2013); The implementation of the Bosnia Status of Forces Agreement was entered in 2005 as a part of NATO Status of Forces Agreement after the UN Mandate expired, comment from; R.Chuck Mason, *Status of Forces Agreement (SOFA), What Is It, and How Has it Been Utilized?* (Washington, D.C.: Congressional Research Service, 2009), CRS-22.

[122]ICMPD, *Financial, Organisational And Administrative Assessment Of The Bih Police Forces And The State Border Service* (Sarajevo: European Union, 2004), 6.

[123]Ibid.

[124]Ibid.

Currently, standard criminal policing and community policing techniques are working in their favor; however, there is the necessity to evaluate their ability to deal with modern cyber and terrorist criminals.[125] Therefore, Bosnia deserves modernization according to the most recent European Union report of Bosnian police forces where the European Union advocates changes for Bosnia to deal with the transforming technologies and the associated crimes.[126] Although, the country has a significant amount of its budget set aside for police salaries, there is a minimal amount reinvested for modernization of the police force.[127] The report also recommended implementing a nationwide salary structure to prevent the disparate payments within the Cantons and prevent corruption.[128]

Iraq

> "The New York City Police Department, managing one of the worlds
> largest training programs, trains 6,000 new officers each year. By comparison, in
> 2003estimates in Iraq were that at least 40,000 completely new police recruits
> would need to be trained and fielded."[129]
> *- Ms. Adrienne Lauzon*

One must first understand Iraq that prior to the United States and coalition invasion of 2003, before assessing the post war efforts for host nation police advising. Prior to March 2003, Iraq, led by Sadam Hussein, was considered secular and a power player in the Middle East. Most of the U. S. Military planners assumed that the infrastructure and systems would be running and

---

[125]ICMPD, *Financial, Organisational And Administrative Assessment Of The Bih Police Forces And The State Border Service* (Sarajevo: European Union, 2004), 6.

[126]Ibid., 9.

[127]ICMPD, *Financial, Organisational And Administrative Assessment Of The Bih Police Forces And The State Border Service*, 2004, 6.

[128]Ibid.

[129]Ms. Adrienne Lauzon, *Local Security, Policing, and Counterinsurgency: Lessons From Iraq* (Norfolk: National Defense University, 2010), 13.

remain running after the invasion, as the military would be precise in targeting.[130] The conventional invasion in March of 2003 only spanned two months and was in fact very precise. Immediately after war, there was calm as forces moved into the cities. This calm, however would not last very long as insurgent undertones began to grow throughout the country.

Following the conventional war, Sadam Hussein and most of the Iraqi Army went into hiding leaving a nation void of security that quickly gave way to looting.[131] Further exasperating this security black hole of government, many government buildings were looted as much of the Iraqi Police abandoned their posts.[132] Glaring examples were the lack of street signs and public officials in the capital of Baghdad. Reports of looting would hinder development in the initial days following the invasion. Examples such as Baghdad's public capacity to make license plates disappeared as the building was looted; however the same license plate machines reappeared in late 2003.[133] Therefore, the war had little effect on the infrastructure, but the poor initial state of the infrastructure and looting of these public facilities affected the post-war situation.[134]

---

[130]James Dobbins et al, *Occupying Iraq: a history of the Coalition Provisional Authority* (Santa Monica: RAND Corporation, 2009), xxvii.

[131]Ibid., xiii.

[132]Ibid., xiii.

[133]Author's personal account from working with the Baghdad Traffic Police in 2003. The traffic police operation that was set up in late 2003, consisted of a round of several stops amongst a courtyard of trailers. In the trailers there was a citizen would stop and file paperwork, then move to payment, then finally receive the license plate, which would be drilled into the Car or automobile. The inspection of the cars would not meet any safety standards of the United States, as a van that was observed through the process had three flat tires and was later driving on the highway with a license plate. Additionally, the plates were strikingly similar to those that were made pre war, indicating a traffic police officer knew exactly where to locate the plate making materials during the months after the looting.

[134]James Dobbins et al, *Occupying Iraq: a history of the Coalition Provisional Authority* (Santa Monica: RAND Corporation, 2009), xxvii; Special Inspector General Report, *Iraqi Security Forces: Police Training Program Developed Sizeable Force, But Capabilities Are Unknown, October 25, 2010*, 1.

Immediate control of Iraq post war was expected to reside in a small number of civilian personnel working with Ambassador Paul Bremer in the Coalition Provisional Authority (CPA). Although Bremer was to administer policy in the absence of the Iraqi Government, he was not in direct control of most of the American Personnel who were a part of the Combined Joint Task Force – 7 (CJTF-7). Bremer made decisions on the cuts and the changes that preceded his entrance into Iraq. The State Department originally planned to send several thousand advisors; however, political disagreements between the White House and the State Department ensued over the arming and quantity of the advisory force.[135] The National Security Council (NSC) staff warned against seeking UN police advisory force.[136] Consequently, the same police advisor force that was relied upon in Bosnia and Kosovo was dismissed during the preparation and planning of Iraq, "on the grounds that [UN police] had proven to be incompetent and corrupt."[137] Many of these decisions would leave CPA without control over advisory resources and fixed with a number of different decisions on security forces.[138] The CPA would rely on personnel like retired New York City Police Commissioner, Bernie Kerik, to assist in those initial decisions. Kerik, however, was not able to bridge the international community with his police experience, which was the beginning of inconsistent policies and strategies to direct the Iraqi Police.[139] In 2004, the responsibility of police development became a Department of Defense's obligation.[140]

---

[135]James Dobbins et al, *Occupying Iraq: a History of the Coalition Provisional Authority* (Santa Monica: RAND Corporation, 2009), xxvii.

[136]Ibid., xxvii, xxv.

[137]Ibid., xxvii, xxv.

[138]Ibid., xxvii.

[139]Ibid., xxvii, xxiv.

[140]Ibid., xxii, xxv; Office of the Special Inspector General for Iraq Reconstruction United States Government, *Iraqi Police Development Program: Opportunities for Improved Program Accountability and Budget Transparency* (Washington, D.C.: U.S. Government, 2011), 1.

Specifically, on May11, 2004, National Security Presidential Directive 362 noted that the DoD Program built a sizeable force that the Iraq Ministry of Interior now oversees and assigns the mission of organizing, training, and equipping Iraq's security forces, including the police, to the U.S. Central Command.[141] Accordingly, as the U.S. Central Command absorbed the obligation for the program there were a number of additional efforts across the United States including external assistance received from multiple nations.

Although the United States Military primarily administered the host nation police advising mission, there was additional support prevalent throughout the myriad of transitional policies and responsibilities. At first in 2003-2004, the Civilian Police Assistance Training Team derived its experience and assistance from numerous screened police officers around the United States to fill its roles.[142] British advisors and the Bureau of Alcohol, Tobacco, Firearms and Explosives also provided advisory capacity from the onset of 2003.[143] Later, as progress in recruitment for the police began, DoD received expertise from the Federal Bureau of Investigation (FBI) and the Department of Homeland Security (DHS) in training.[144] They sought

---

[141]Office of the Special Inspector General for Iraq Reconstruction United States Government, *Iraqi Police Development Program: Opportunities for Improved Program Accountability and Budget Transparency* (Washington, D.C.: U.S. Government, 2011), 1.

[142]Center of Army Lessons Learned, *Zero to Blue Special Study* (Ft. Leavenworth: Ft. Leavenworth Press, 2007), 1; Civilian Police Assistance Training Team was authorized over 790 personnel to assist in developing a 135,000 Iraqi Police force.

[143]Office of the Special Inspector General for Iraq Reconstruction United States Government, *Iraqi Police Development Program: Opportunities for Improved Program Accountability and Budget Transparency* (Washington, D.C.: U.S. Government, 2011),3; Center of Army Lessons Learned, *Zero to Blue Special study* (Ft. Leavenworth: Ft. Leavenworth Press, 2007), 1; Office of the Special Inspector General, *Iraqi Security Forces: Police Training Program Developed Sizeable Force, But Capabilities Are Unknown* (Washington, D.C.: U.S. Government, 2010), 6.

[144]Office of the Special Inspector General for Iraq Reconstruction United States Government, *Iraqi Police Development Program: Opportunities for Improved Program Accountability and Budget Transparency* (Washington, D.C.:U.S. Government, 2011), 3.

expertise for specific skills such as investigations and border security.[145] Most of the advisory

force was comprised of military police officers with investigator experience that varied amongst

ranks.[146] Often the Military Police forces had various reserve elements that also served as police

officers in local state and county precincts, and were very effective in various policing

techniques.[147] All of these efforts, brought a diverse mixture of experience to the police advisory

mission however, it also produced inconsistency.[148]

At its final stages the advisory mission morphed into the Iraq Training and Advisory

Mission (ITAM). ITAM fulfilled the larger responsibility of synchronizing the advisory efforts of

all entities.[149] This included synchronizing the Military with the Military Police Transition Team

efforts that were at the lower levels with the Iraqi Police.[150] The ITAM also worked to

synchronize the efforts of the Ministry of Interior (MoI), as it was able to take on a stronger role

in controlling and administering policy for its police force.[151] After 2010, the Department of State

---

[145]Office of the Special Inspector General for Iraq Reconstruction United States Government, *Iraqi Police Development Program: Opportunities for Improved Program Accountability and Budget Transparency* (Washington, D.C.: U.S. Government, 2011), 3.

[146]Center of Army Lessons Learned, *Zero to Blue Special Study* (Ft. Leavenworth, KS: Ft. Leavenworth Press, 2007), 2.

[147]Ibid.

[148]Ibid., 1.

[149]Office of the Special Inspector General, *Iraqi Security Forces: Police Training Program Developed Sizeable Force, But Capabilities Are Unknown* (Washington, D.C.: U.S. Government, 2010), 2-6.

[150]Ibid., 2.

[151]Office of the Special Inspector General for Iraq Reconstruction United States Government, *Iraqi Police Development Program: Opportunities for Improved Program Accountability and Budget Transparency* (Washington, D.C.: U.S. Government, 2011), 2.

assumed the role of advising the police force in Iraq.[152] More importantly, this program is now less than 190 advisors in only ten of the eighteen provinces.[153]

The development and transitions of the advisory mission preceded the transition in the Iraqi police force. The Iraq police force prior to the invasion in March of 2003 was estimated at strength of 58,000.[154] Ambassador Bremer decided to keep the police force and structure intact, however, this force would take years to mature.[155] Consequently, the structure of the Iraqi police force would remain divided amongst eighteen provinces and controlled at the national level by the Iraqi MoI. Although the structure was to remain, there was neither a force nor the public officials to run it at the official end of the war in 2010.

As the police force was beginning to rebuild, the forces would increase dramatically in numbers, however the capabilities were debatable.[156] The current numbers for the Iraqi Police extend beyond 400,000 police officers, with the last DoD report stating there are 412,000.[157] The Iraqi Ministry of Interior currently manages fifteen of the provinces.[158] Moreover, the Ministry of

---

[152]Office of the Special Inspector General for Iraq Reconstruction United States Government, *Iraqi Police Development Program: Opportunities for Improved Program Accountability and Budget Transparency* (Washington, D.C.: U.S. Government, 2011), 9.

[153]Ibid., 9.

[154]Ibid., 1-2.

[155]James Dobbins et al, *Occupying Iraq: A history of the Coalition Provisional Authority* (Santa Monica: RAND Corporation, 2009), xxi.

[156]Ibid., xxv.

[157]Office of the Special Inspector General, *Iraqi Security Forces: Police Training Program Developed Sizeable Force, But Capabilities Are Unknown* (Washington, D.C.: U.S. Government, 2010), x; Office of the Special Inspector General for Iraq Reconstruction United States Government, *Iraqi Police Development Program: Opportunities for Improved Program Accountability and Budget Transparency* (Washington, D.C.: U.S. Government, 2011), 1-2.

[158]Office of the Special Inspector General for Iraq Reconstruction United States Government, *Iraqi Police Development Program: Opportunities for Improved Program Accountability and Budget Transparency* (Washington, D.C.: U.S. Government, 2011), 1- 2.

Interior runs a number of additional services such as the Federal Police, the Border Patrol, the Federal Protection Services and the Oil Police.[159] The Ministry assumed the direction for the police training as early as 2006 of which they currently administer five police colleges and thirty-two training centers.[160]

Concurrent to the rebuilding of the police force was the reestablishment of the Iraqi judicial system. The system remained incomplete, just as the Iraqi Police structure did in 2003. The court system was the same system that completed a record caseload in 2004, as well as successfully adjudicated over Sadam Hussein's trial.[161] The European Union was among one of the many that assisted these programs that helped the Ministry of Interior in concurrent development.[162]

The Iraqi Criminal Justice system and enforcement arms of the Iraqi Police are established and currently at a higher capacity than before the war, however, this has not been without scrutiny. There was scrutiny over the Coalition Provisional Authority for growing the Iraqi Police Force at the expense of capability and quality of the police.[163] The Special Inspector General for Iraq Reconstruction, stated numerous times in reports that they do not have an

---

[159]Office of the Special Inspector General, *Iraqi Security Forces: Police Training Program Developed Sizeable Force, But Capabilities Are Unknown* (Washington, D.C.: U.S. Government, 2010), 3.

[160]Office of the Special Inspector General for Iraq Reconstruction United States Government, *Iraqi Police Development Program: Opportunities for Improved Program Accountability and Budget Transparency* (Washington, D.C.: U.S. Government, 2011), 2.

[161]James Dobbins et al, *Occupying Iraq: A History of the Coalition Provisional Authority* (Santa Monica: RAND Corporation, 2009), xxx.

[162]Office of the Special Inspector General, *Iraqi Security Forces: Police Training Program Developed Sizeable Force, But Capabilities Are Unknown* (Washington, D.C.: U.S. Government, 2010), 6.

[163]James Dobbins et al, *Occupying Iraq: A History of the Coalition Provisional Authority* (Santa Monica: RAND Corporation, 2009), xxv.

accurate assessment of the current Iraqi Police capability.[164] Furthermore, both the Inspector General office and external Rand references depicted inconclusive standards based on the lack of metrics. These assessments, however, are seen through the eyes of the beholder and do not explain the zones of tolerance for the establishment of the Iraq police force.[165]

Just as in the previous conflicts of Bosnia and Germany, the length of stay of the force post conflict is greatly determined by the parameters for which one defines. Sources may include the years from 2003-2011 as the conflict, however, for the process of consistency amongst the studies, the stability phase begins for comparison of this study as 2003. May 2003 marked the completion of major combat fighting.[166] The negotiations for a security agreement began as early as 2007; however, it was not signed until 2008 after congressional approval.[167] This negotiation required the withdrawal of U.S. Soldiers by December 31, 2011.[168] As discussed earlier, there are still host nation police advising roles being fulfilled by the United States State Department that began in October of 2011.[169]

---

[164]Office of the Special Inspector General for Iraq Reconstruction United States Government, *Iraqi Police Development Program: Opportunities for Improved Program Accountability and Budget Transparency*, (Washington, D.C.: U.S. Government, 2011), 1-2; Office of the Special Inspector General, *Iraqi Security Forces: Police Training Program Developed Sizeable Force, But Capabilities Are Unknown*, (Washington, D.C.: U.S. Government, 2010), x.

[165]James Dobbins et al, *Occupying Iraq: A History of the Coalition Provisional Authority* (Santa Monica: RAND Corporation, 2009), xxv.

[166]James Rosen, "Bush Says Major Combat in Iraq is Over," Fox News, 2 May 2003, http://www.foxnews.com/story/0,2933,85777,00.html, (accessed 1 April 2013).

[167]R.Chuck Mason, *Status of Forces Agreement (SOFA), What Is It, and How Has it Been Utilized?* (Washington, D.C.: Congressional Research Service, 2009),15.

[168]Ibid.

[169]Office of the Special Inspector General for Iraq Reconstruction United States Government, *Iraqi Police Development Program: Opportunities for Improved Program Accountability and Budget Transparency*, (Washington, D.C.: U.S. Government, 2011), 2-3.

ANALYSIS

This portion of the research synthesizes the main points that appeared throughout the case studies of Germany, Bosnia, and Iraq. Comparing the national level government and the differences of conflicts between Germany, Bosnia, and Iraq will provide the baseline for determining where the countries differ. Additional analysis of the police advisory force in each country and the known outcomes are to gleam valuable lessons that illustrate possible future solutions.

Democracy is determined as a factor that affects future solutions in nation building. What is significant to the case study analysis is the level of the pre-conflict democratic nation to the length of the advisory force stay. For example, post WWI Germany illustrates where USAID's policy or a civilian advisory force would work from the onset, as it was already an unstable democracy before the rise of Nazism.[170] This may also explain the quick transition from the U.S. Constabulary to the Germany Police in 1947, just two years after the American occupation as the population understood and accepted the tenets requisite of a democratic system. Furthermore, the short amount of years that the Constabulary had to enforce laws is based on the strong foundation of rule of law and police structure that Germany had to reestablish and not build. Whereas, Bosnia and Iraq had a significant police structure rebuilt post conflict and no exposure to democratic policies until post conflict; therefore, requiring a longer host nation police advisory mission.

All three countries had minimal police forces left after the war, as well as damaged public infrastructure that affected the police forces abilities within the stability phase. All three countries maintained semblances to previous institutional configurations but built upon the structure of the

---

[170]United States Agency for International Development, *Assistance for Civilian Policing.*USAID Policy Guidance, 2005, vi.

36

local police. Furthermore, all the additional structure was in conjunction with the expansion of the laws. These expansions were simultaneous to the major changes in the National Government's policies and constitution.

Another similarity between the case studies is the decisions to maintain the police and not to totally disband them. Although all three countries maintained a similar pre-war police configuration, they necessitated a de-Nazification and de-Bathafication processes while demobilizing the Armed Forces in each country. For example, "after the peacekeeping forces began to realize the demobilization process was bloating the police forces beyond the European standards, the process stopped."[171] All three case studies illustrate the direct impacts the demobilization of the military has on the police forces. These unintended consequences should shape the lessons for future of stability operations and deserve further investigation as they are outside the scope of the current intended study.

This study notes the contrasting differences of the advisory forces within the nations. Post war Germany had a U.S. Military led advisory force that remained for only a few years. In Bosnia, The role of the IPTF was distinctly different from that of the German post conflict Constabulary of the 1940s. The task force filled a direct training and advising mission from the beginning but was a "hodgepodge" of unarmed police officers with various experience and backgrounds.[172] As the Department of Defense superseded the State Departments recommendation for a civilian advisory force in Iraq, the force was mostly comprised of the U.S.

---

[171]Larry K. Wentz, *Lessons from Bosnia* (Washington D.C.: National Defense University Press, 1997), 14; The European Standard for police force ratio was one police officer per 330 persons, however the military forces that joined the Police exceeded that ratio.

[172]James Dobbins, John G. McGinn, Keith Crane, Seth G. Jones, Rollie Lal, Andrew Rathmell, Rachel Swanger, and Anga Timilsina, *America's Role in Nation-Building: From Germany to Iraq* (Santa Monica: RAND Corporation, 2003), 97-98.

Military Police Force in Iraq in 2003. This advisory force in Iraq became a Department of Defense led operation with civilian complementary efforts.

The most complicated measurement of comparison is in the outcomes of the efforts of these advisory forces. Germany is an international leader that assists in advising other police forces. Although the police advisory was only a part of building Germany's well-buffered system, Germany's police are a critical part of the countries security. Bosnian Police forces have withstood the ethnic divides and they are meeting European standards.[173] Although the U.S. State Department is still maintaining a police advisory effort in Iraq they claim that the Police capacity is unknown in the nation. The country may be fragile but Iraq has not fallen since the U.S. military has pulled out. Furthermore, Iraq had an increase of over 350,000 police officers trained while the Department of Defense was responsible for advising the Iraqi police over the course of eight years.

This study continues to unfold with the continuation of the State Department advisor program and the State Department assessment of the Iraqi police capabilities. Both a recent Inspector General and the Rand Corporation publication referenced inconclusive standards based on the lack of metrics in Iraq, however, these are the American narrative.[174] Neither report explains the zones of tolerance, or the objective for the establishment of the Iraq police force. In comparison, the Bosnian IPTF left in 2002, however, the Bosnian capability studies were not available until 2004. As a result, we may see the capability assessments within the immediate years following 2013. What is certain is the fact that Iraq Government invoked their sovereignty

---

[173]ICMPD, *Financial, Organisational And Administrative Assessment Of The Bih Police Forces And The State Border Service* (Sarajevo: European Union, 2004), 6.

[174]James Dobbins et al, *Occupying Iraq: A history of the Coalition Provisional Authority* (Santa Monica, CA: RAND Corporation, 2009), xxv; Office of the Special Inspector General, *Iraqi Security Forces: Police Training Program Developed Sizeable Force, But Capabilities Are Unknown* (Washington, D.C.: U.S. Government, 2010).

rights with the implementation of the SOFA and they are now responsible for their outcome as opposed to an occupational authority. Therefore, Iraq is now responsible for policing their own population.

What is consistently noted is the ideals that each of the police forces and occupational authorities desired and the numerous amounts of opinions and setbacks each force encountered as they conducted their roles. Each force was criticized for the way it conducted business regardless of how the force was employed. [175] There appears to be no secret to each success, but rather a steady pursuit to make the police force better adherent to human rights standards. The nation's previous exposure to democratic views and ideology, their security situation, and the amount of the police institution that remained were the contingent factors in the type of advisory force recommended.

CONCLUSION

Promoting a prescriptive police advising force appeals to be ideal, however, there is good reason as discovered through the literature review and the case studies now for not prescribing a force. Accordingly, each case study was successful to various degrees but that success depended upon the state of their government prior to the conflict. Germany was the only country that was exposed to democratic ideals prior to the conflict. Therefore, Bosnia and Iraq both required a change in the national level structure while simultaneously adjusting and expanding the police force capacity. Consequently, the research is suspect of any prescriptive force for a stability operation, as every stability operation is dependent upon a varied degree of the national cohesion and where the zone of tolerance is for democratic or community policing in that nation. For

---

[175]Kendall D. Gott and Combat Studies Institute, *Mobility, Vigilance, and Justice: the U.S. Army Constabulary in Germany 1946-1953* (Ft. Leavenworth: Combat Studies Institute Press, 2005), 1.

instance, Melissa Cantwell prescribes that the United States Military Police Corps must have more investigative and police specialized training in order to be successful in advising.[176] The broader aspect, however, is that the current capacity of a nation and its exposure to democracy must precede the choosing of the host nation's police advising force. In essence, the nation's capacity affects the composition of the advisory force more than any other factor.

The following model describes the nation's current capacity within zones of tolerance to reach a community policing or proactive type police force. In analysis of policy, documents and journals from the literature review the intent of providing police or constabulary advisement ranges along a spectrum of democratic police to community police functions.

Spectrum of United States Host Nation Policing

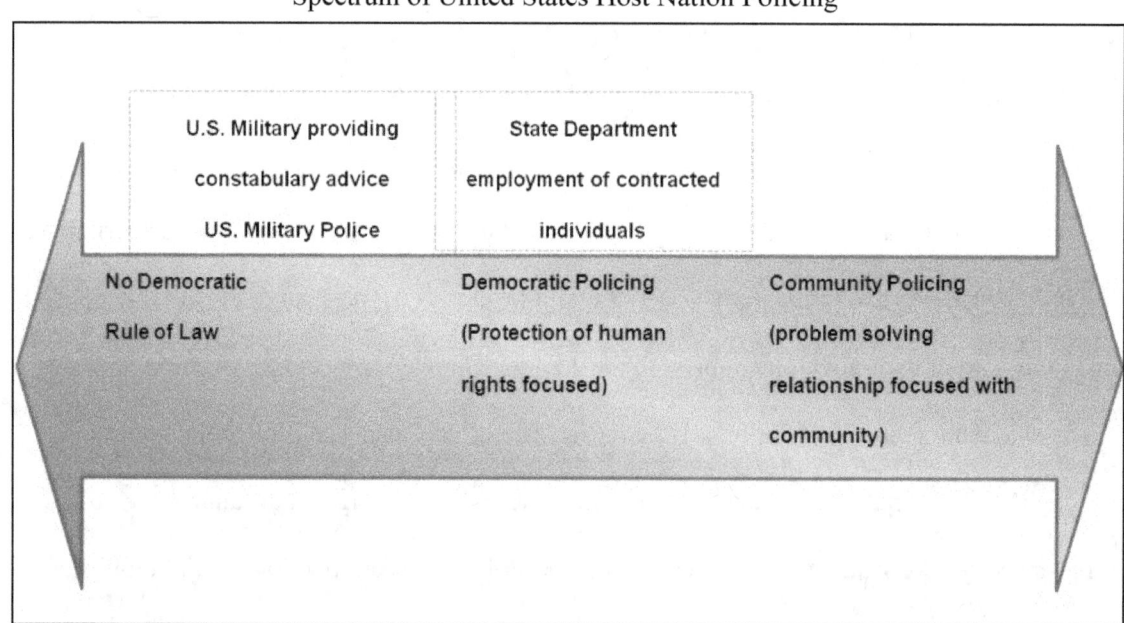

Chart made by Major Christine Baker to reflect the varying degrees of host nation policing.

---

[176]Melissa M. Cantwell, *"Evolution of Both Host Nation Police Advisory and the Support Provided by the Department of Defense,"* (Master's Thesis, School of Advanced Military Studies, 2012), 60-63.

Community policing emerges as the ideal standard that many scholars recommend, however, the United Nations and USAID recommend an international standard of human rights recognition for police forces. Imposing international standards such as community policing on other nations is extremely hard for a country that does not nationally standardize community policing. For example, American police accreditation was established in 1979, yet most of the nation's police forces retain their professional criterion at the state level.[177] For that reason, how can a nation try to impose standards that their own nation does not follow nor do they necessarily propose nationally? Accordingly, future planners could recommend a community-policing standard that understands the system that they recommend has a number of complex factors that will force the advisory function into zones of tolerance and not into a singular nationally defined function.

The study must further be conducted on the presence of the military and the amount of aid that is put into the nation. Additionally, this research recommends a study of the correlation of the judicial process in each of these case studies in comparison of the judicial process on the advisory of police forces. Further evaluation is also necessary upon the completion of Iraq metrics, which may become available in the upcoming years. Additional evaluation should also be done on host nation police advising on the number of other nations that the United States has assisted in post-conflict to include Afghanistan, Panama, Kosovo, S. Korea, and Japan. Although there is certainly room for future studies, this research concludes that there is a time for military advisory and a time to implement a USAID police advisory force.

---

[177]CALEA, "CALEA recognizes 87 public safety agencies," http://www.calea.org/content/law-enforcement-accreditation (accessed 8 February 2013)

BIBLIOGRAPHY

Center of Army Lessons Learned. (2007). *From Zero to Blue Special Study: Civilian Police Assistance Training.* Fort Leavenworth, KS: Fort Leavenworth Press.

Biglan, A., Ary, D., & Alexander, C. W. (2000). The Value of Interupted Time Series Experiments For Community Intervention Research. *Prevention Science* , 31-49.

Bureau of Justice Assistance. (1994). "Understanding Community Policing: A Framework for Action." *Community Policing Consortium* (pp. 1-82). Washington, D.C.: U.S. Department of Justice.

CALEA. (2012, March 29). *CALEA recognizes 87 public safety agencies.* CALEA: http://www.calea.org/content/law-enforcement-accreditation (accessed 8 February 2013).

Cantwell, M. M. "Evolution of Both Host Nation Police Advisory and the Support Provided by the Department of Defense." Fort Leavenworth: School of Advanced Military Studies, 2012.

Casey, G. W. (2012). *Strategic Reflections: Operation Iraqi Freedom.* Washington, D.C.: National Defense University Press.

Connable, B., & Libicki, M. C. (2010). *How Insurgencies End.* Santa Monica: RAND Corportaion.

Dobbins, J. (2009). *Occupying Iraq: A History of the Coalition Provisional Authority.* Santa Monica, CA: RAND Corporation.

Dobbins, J., Mcginn, J. G., Crane, K., Jones, S. G., Lal, R., Rathmell, A., et al. (2003). *America's Role in Nation-Building: From Germany to Iraq.* Santa Monica, Calif.: RAND Corporation.

Evans, R. J. (2005). *The Third Reich in Power.* New York, NY: Penguin Books.

Fillingham, Z. (4 July 2012). *Nation Building & Police Reform: Lessons from Georgia.* from Geopolitical Monitor: http://www.geopoliticalmonitor.com/nation-building-police-reform-lessons-from-georgia-4696 (Accessed 3 December 2012).

Frederiksen, O. F. (1984). *The American Military Occupation of Germany 1945-1953.* Heidelberg, Germany: U.S. Army Europe.

Friedmann, R. R., & Cannon, W. J. (2007). "Homeland Security and Community Policing: Competing or Complementing Public Safety Policies." *Journal of Homeland Security and Emergency Management* 4, no. 4, pp. 1-23.

Galula, D. (1964). *Counter-Insurgency Warfare: Theory and Practice.* New York: Frederick A. Praeger, Inc.

Gott, K., & Institute, C. S. (2005). *Mobility, Vigilance, and Justice: the U.S. Army Constabulary in Germany, 1946-1953: Global War on Terrorism Occasional Paper 11.* Fort Leavenworth, Kansas: Combat Studies Institute Press.

Grayling, A. (2006). *Among the Dead Cities: The History and Moral Legacy of the WWII Bombing Campaign of Civilians in Germany and Japan.* New York, NY: Walker & Company.

Historical Division European Command. (1950). *Reorganization of Tactical Forces VE-Day to 1 January 1949.* Karlsrule, Germany: European Command.

Horgan, Edward J. "Assisting or Hindering Democracy? International Intervention and the Democratisation of Bosnia and Herzegovina." Dissertation. Master of Philosophy in Peace Studies, Irish School of Ecumenics, 1999.

ICMPD. (2004). Financial, Organizational And Administrative Assessment of The BIH Police Forces and the State Border Service. Sarajevo: European Union.

International Crisis Group. "Policing the Police in Bosnia: A Further Reform Agenda." *Balkans Report N°130, Sarajevo/Brussels*, 10 May 2002. http://www.crisisgroup.org/en/regions/europe/balkans/bosnia-herzegovina/130-policing-the-police-in-bosnia-a-further-reform-agenda.aspx, (accessed 3 March 2013).

Johnson, T. D. (2007). *A Gallant Little Army, The Mexico City Campaign.* Lawrence: University Press of Kansas.

Jones, S., Wilson, J. M., Rathmell, A., & Riley, K. J. (2005). *Establishing Law and Order After Conflict.* Santa Monica, CA: RAND Corporation.

Keller, D. E. (2010). *U.S. Military Forces and Police Assistance in Stability Operations: The Least-Worst Option to Fill the U.S. Capacity Gap.* Carlisle: Strategic Studies Institute.

Lauzon, A. (2010). *Local Security, Policing, and Counterinsurgency: Lessons From Iraq.* Norfolk, VA.: National Defense University.

Marlowe, A. "David Galula: His Life and Intellectual Context." Monograph. U.S. War College, Department of the Army, 2010.

Office of the Special Inspector General for Iraq Reconstruction. (2010) *Iraqi Police Development Program: opportunitities for Improved Program Accountability and Budget Transparency,* Washington, DC: U.S. Government.

---. (2011). *Police Training Program Developed Sizeable Force, But Capabilities are Unknown.* Washington, DC: U.S. Government.

R. Chuck Mason. (18 July 2009). *Status of Forces Agreement (SOFA), What is It, and How has It Been Utilized?* Washington, DC: Congressional Research Service.

Reynolds, P. D. (1971). *Primer in Theory Construction.* Boston: Allyn and Bacon.

Rosen, James. "Bush Says Major Combat in Iraq is Over", Fox News, 2 May 2003. http://www.foxnews.com/story/0,2933,85777,00.html, (accessed 1 April 2013).

Snyder, M. J. (1947). E*stablishment Operations of the U.S. Constabulary 3 October 1945 to 30 June 1947.* APO, Germany,: U.S. Army.

United States Agency for International Development. (2005). *Assistance for Civilian Policing.* Washington, DC: United States Agency for International Development.

U.S. Army. (2012). Army Doctrine Publication 3-0, *Operations.* Washington DC: Headquarters, Department of the Army.

Wentz, L. (1997). *Bosnia Lessons Learned.* Washington DC: National Defense University Press.

Wither, J. K. (2012). Challenges of Developing Host Nation Police Capacity. *Prism* 4, no. 3, pp. 39-53.

Wright, R. K. (1992). *Military Police.* Washington, D.C. 1992: Center of Military History.

Young, K. (2001, September). UNHCR and ICRC in the Former. *RICR* , pp. 781-805.

APPENDIX A: DEFINITIONS

Community Policing -Values the level of involvement of the community and the proactive means a police force takes to solve community problems.[178]

Democratic Police - Police force work under a democratic rule of law, enforce human rights and are subject to assessment.[179]

Host Nation Police Advising - Foreign advising of a police force.

Martial Law - Enforcing the rule of law over a nation with the use of a military.

Police State - Harsh enforcement by a police force or a military force to control a society for establishment of a significantly harsher values system.

---

[178]Bureau of Justice Assistance, "Understanding Community Policing: A Framework for Action." *Community Policing Consortium.* (Washington, D.C.: U.S. Department of Justice,1994),1-82; Robert R Friedmann, William J. Cannon. "Homeland Security and Community Policing: Competing or Complementing Public Safety Policies". *Journal of Homeland Security and Emergency Management* 4, no. 4, (2007)1-23.

[179]United States Agency for International Development, *Assistance for Civilian Policing.USAID Policy Guidance*, (Washington, D.C.: United States Agency for International Development: 2005),V.

www.ingramcontent.com/pod-product-compliance
Lightning Source LLC
Chambersburg PA
CBHW080618290526
45790CB00007B/2828